God Made Fish

Draw a circle around the butterfly that is different.

Family Time

In this lesson the children talked about surprises God put in our world—in particular, lovely butterflies that come from caterpillars. This prepares the children for the dramatic change we make at death when we enter into new eternal life. Have your child talk about the surprises pictured on this card and tell you the story of a butterfly's life. Display the picture your child made in class.

The life cycle of a butterfly and the death of a seed that is born again as a flower are symbols and promises of our new life. As Jesus rose from the dead, so will we. This mystery is beyond the scope of our understanding. Answer your child's questions about death simply and honestly. Because of Jesus' resurrection we can rejoice in this life in preparation for the next.

Suggested activities
* Point out natural wonders, such as rainbows.
* Take your child to a natural history museum. Convey wonder over the world's marvels.
* Take a nature walk with your child and admire God's gifts.
* Plant seeds with your child and watch them grow.
* Pray a litany with your child. Name wonders of the world and respond, "Praise the LORD, who is so good" (Psalm 136:1).
* Read to your child *The Very Hungry Caterpillar* by Eric Carle.

Name

God Made Butterflies

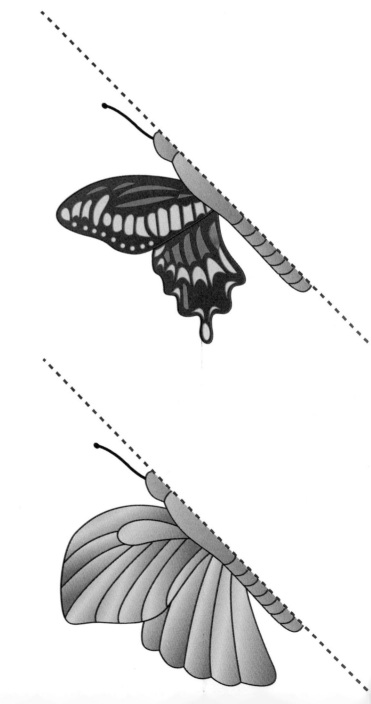

God Made Butterflies

God Made the World

Draw something you have seen that is very large.

Family Time

In this lesson the children considered some of God's huge creations, such as oceans, mountains, and dinosaurs. They learned that God is very great and powerful. They also heard that God loves them more than these great things. Read or have your child tell you about his or her book about God's love. Ask your child about the giant thank-you card the class made for God.

A valuable lesson for children is that through cooperation great things can be accomplished. Point out to your child the advantages of having a task done by a group.

Suggested activities
- Have several children work together to make cookies.
- If possible, take your child where he or she can experience a large natural creation, such as a river, lake, mountain, or plain.
- Have your child share the story of God's love by "reading" the book about it to someone.
- Help your child draw a very large picture.
- Affirm family members. Sit in a circle on the floor. Choose someone to spin a bottle and tell how God's love is shown through the person to whom the bottle points. That person then spins the bottle.
- Read to your child *The Story of Babar* by Jean de Brunhoff or *Whale Song* by Tony Johnston.

Name

stronger than a lion.

And God loves me!

4

My Book about God's Great Love

God's love is higher than a mountain,

1

wider than the sky,

deeper than the ocean,

bigger than a whale,

2

3

God Made Big Things

God Made the World

Circle the seven little creatures hidden in the picture.

God Made Little Things

Family Time

In this lesson the children focused on small things that God made. They learned to value small living things and praised God for them. They saw the potential of small things, such as acorns and babies. Ask your child to show you the pet pocket made in class.

Children can appreciate the ingenuity of the Creator by examining the intricacies of small, delicate creations. Often during walks children will stop abruptly, absorbed by some small thing.

Suggested activities
- Study an ant or another small thing with your child. Point out its features and special powers.
- Show your child his or her baby pictures. Call attention to the tiny fingernails and toes.
- Look at several small things with your child through a magnifying glass.
- Provide your child with a special box for small treasures.
- Read to your child *Be Nice to Spiders* by Margaret B. Graham or *Go and Hush the Baby* by Betsy Byars.

Name _____

Pet Pocket

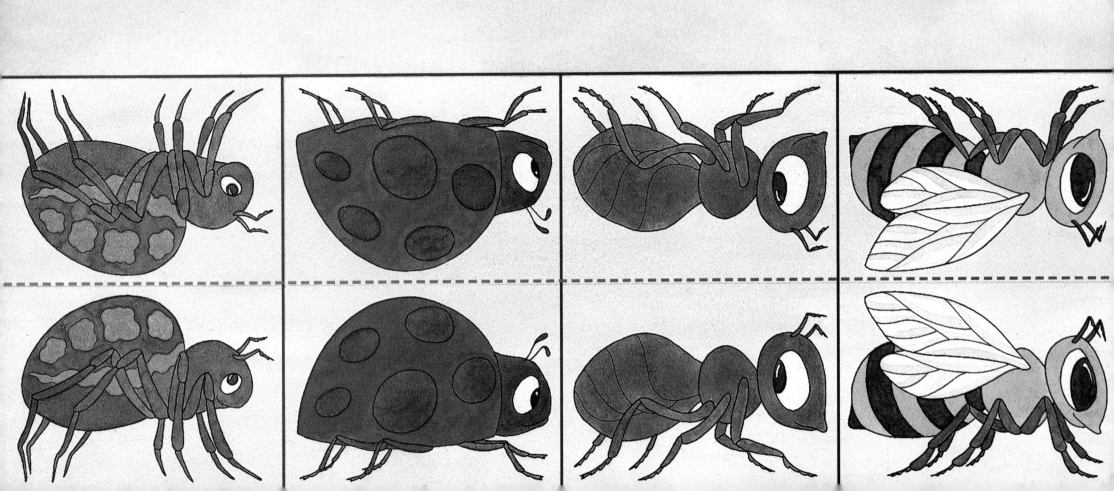

God Made the World

Draw a line from each child to the heart.

Family Time

In this lesson the children were made aware of the many different countries that make up the world. They learned that although people in these countries may look different, eat different things, and have different customs, they are all human beings. They were led to regard others as their brothers and sisters in the family of God. Find out about the country whose flag your child made. Tell your child about it.

Prejudice is learned quickly by children. Help your child come to respect other people by introducing him or her to people of different races and nationalities.

Suggested activities
- Invite people from another country to come to your house for dinner.
- Try recipes from other countries.
- Point out to your child some accomplishments of people from other nations.
- Pray together for people in other countries who need our prayers.
- Read to your child *A Country Far Away* by Nigel Gray.

Name _____

God Made Countries

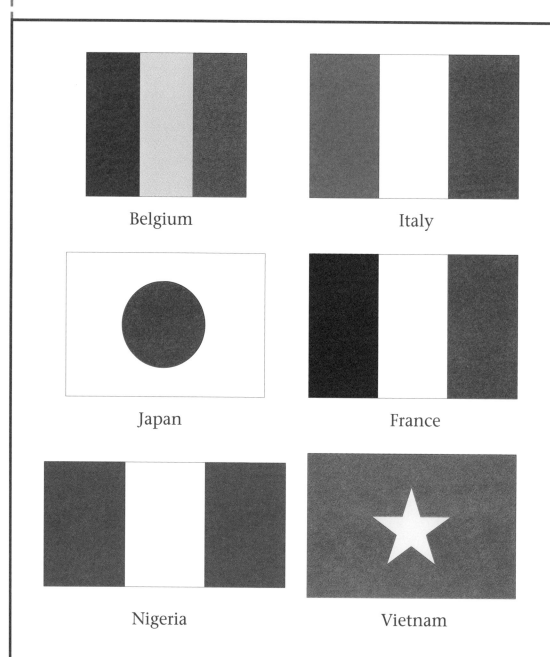

Belgium

Italy

Japan

France

Nigeria

Vietnam

God Made Countries

What do you think is funny?

Family Time

In this lesson the children learned that God wants us to be happy and that being close to God makes us happy. They talked about ways to make other people happy. Suggest that your child wear the clown hat made in class whenever he or she feels sad.

One of the best ways to be happy is to make someone else happy. Do something with your child to surprise someone and make that person happy.

Suggested activities
- Enjoy a comical television program or movie with your child.
- Share jokes with your child.
- Do something to make your child happy.
- Tell your child a funny story.
- Plan summer activities that would be fun for everyone in the family.
- Read to your child *The Seven Chinese Brothers* by Margaret Mahy or *Tommy at the Grocery Store* by Bill Grossman.

Name _____

God Made Laughter

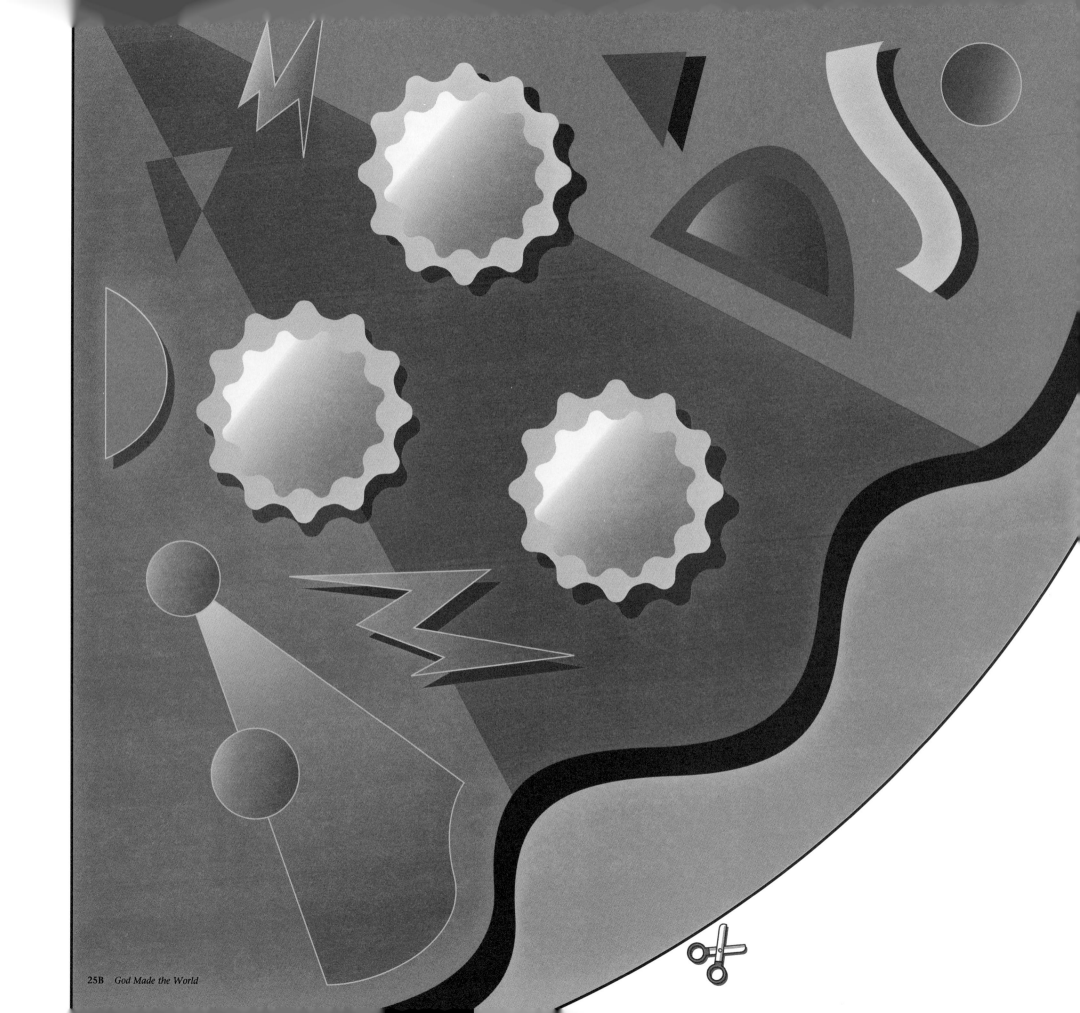

Family Time

In this lesson the children celebrated their birthdays. They recalled that their life is a gift from God. Ask your child to show you the book about life made in class. Have him or her tell you about it.

A birthday is an occasion to enhance your child's self-concept. Birthdays celebrate the person. Make your child's birthday something special. Include a special prayer thanking God for the gift of your child to your family.

Suggested activities
- Look at pictures with your child that show how much he or she has grown.
- Have a birthday party and invite your child's friends.
- Serve your child's favorite food on his or her birthday.
- Show your child his or her birth certificate, bronzed shoes, hair from his or her first haircut, or other mementoes of the beginning of life.
- Occasionally celebrate half-birthdays of family members.
- Hang a banner or flag on the house in honor of your child's birthday.
- Read to your child *On the Day You Were Born* by Debra Fraser.

Decorate the cake. Add flames to the candles.

Name

I Thank God I'm Alive!

I can see sunsets and skyscrapers,
daisies and stars,
and people who love me.

1

I can hear music, wind in the trees,
raindrops on the roof,
and my mother calling me.

2

I can feel a kitten's fur,
the warm sun,
and a hug.

3

I can run down the street,
into the lake,
or to Grandma's house.

4

I can eat turkey, pizza, peas,
  chocolate chip cookies,
    strawberries,
      and popcorn.

7

I'm alive and I'm five.
Life is great. Let's celebrate.

8

I can shout for joy,
whisper a secret,
and sing a song.

5

I can play hide-and-seek,
watch movies, feed ducks,
and snuggle under blankets on a cold night.

6

Color the pieces orange that have a dot.

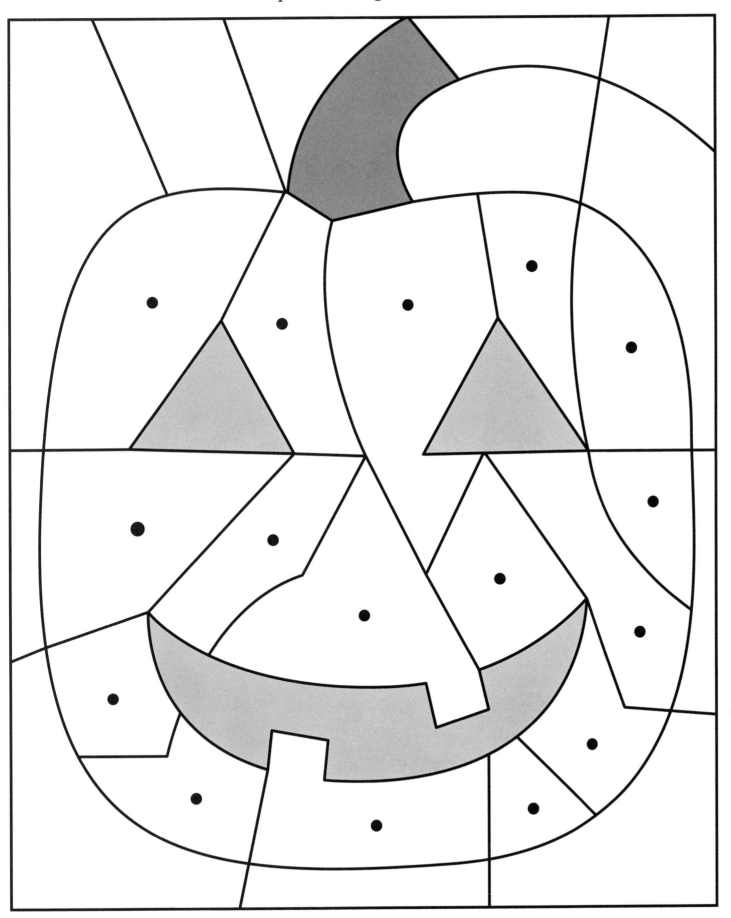

Family Time

In this lesson the children learned that Halloween is the night before we celebrate All Saints Day. They heard the story of St. Elizabeth of Hungary and were invited to let God's love shine from them as Elizabeth did. They were encouraged to show love by smiling. Ask your child why a crown was made in class.

For children Halloween should be a night of fun in safe surroundings. You might hold a party at your house on Halloween for your child and friends.

Suggested activities
- Carve a pumpkin with the help of your child.
- Tell your child about his or her patron saint.
- Make a special bag to hold treats for your child.
- Read to your child *Which Witch Is Which?* by Pat Hutchins or *Pumpkin, Pumpkin* by Jeanne Titherington.

Name _____

Halloween

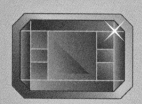

ST._____

Halloween

Color the ★ pieces 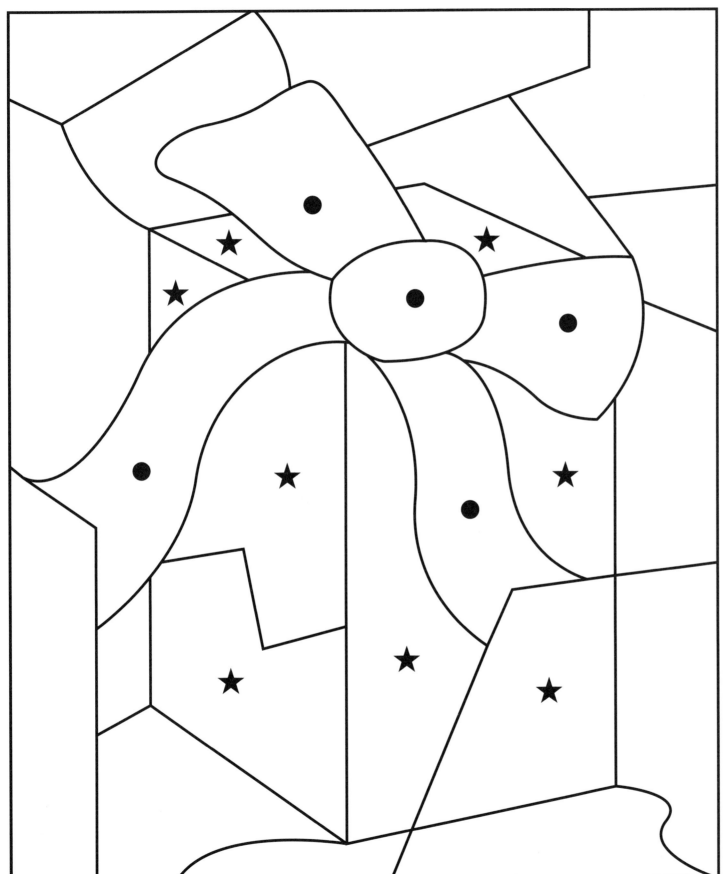 and the ● pieces .

Family Time

In this lesson the children learned that we prepare for Jesus' birthday by being kind and loving. The children made a manger and will put a piece of "straw" into it for every good act. Suggest acts that your child is able to do.

Christmas is usually a child's first introduction to Jesus. Take advantage of this feast to talk about Jesus, Mary, and Joseph.

Suggested activities
- Set up a manger scene at home.
- Take your child with you to deliver food and clothing to people who need them.
- Join a group of Christmas carolers with your child.
- Help your child make homemade gifts for family members.
- Have a prayer service to bless your Christmas tree and/or your manger scene. *Catholic Household Blessings and Prayers*, published by the Bishop's Committee on the Liturgy, offers many ideas for family prayers, such as these Christmas blessings.
- Read to your child *On the Way to Bethlehem* by C. M. DeVries.

Name

Advent

God Made the World

Draw something you thank God for.

Thank you, God

Family Time

In this lesson the children learned that Thanksgiving Day is a day to thank God. They made a thank-you card for God. Incorporate the stand-up turkey your child made in your Thanksgiving Day dinner centerpiece.

Let your child see and hear you praying in thanksgiving to God.

Suggested activities
- Invite a person to your Thanksgiving dinner who otherwise might not have a big meal.
- Take your child with you to deliver food or clothing for the poor or to help serve dinners for the poor.
- Let your child help with your Thanksgiving dinner.
- Prepare a special prayer for your Thanksgiving meal. Everyone around the table might express gratitude for one thing.
- Plan to celebrate the Eucharist as a family on Thanksgiving Day.
- Read to your child *Sometimes It's Turkey—Sometimes It's Feathers* by Lorna Balian or *Silly Tilly's Thanksgiving Dinner* by Lillian Hoban.

Name _____

Happy
Thanksgiving

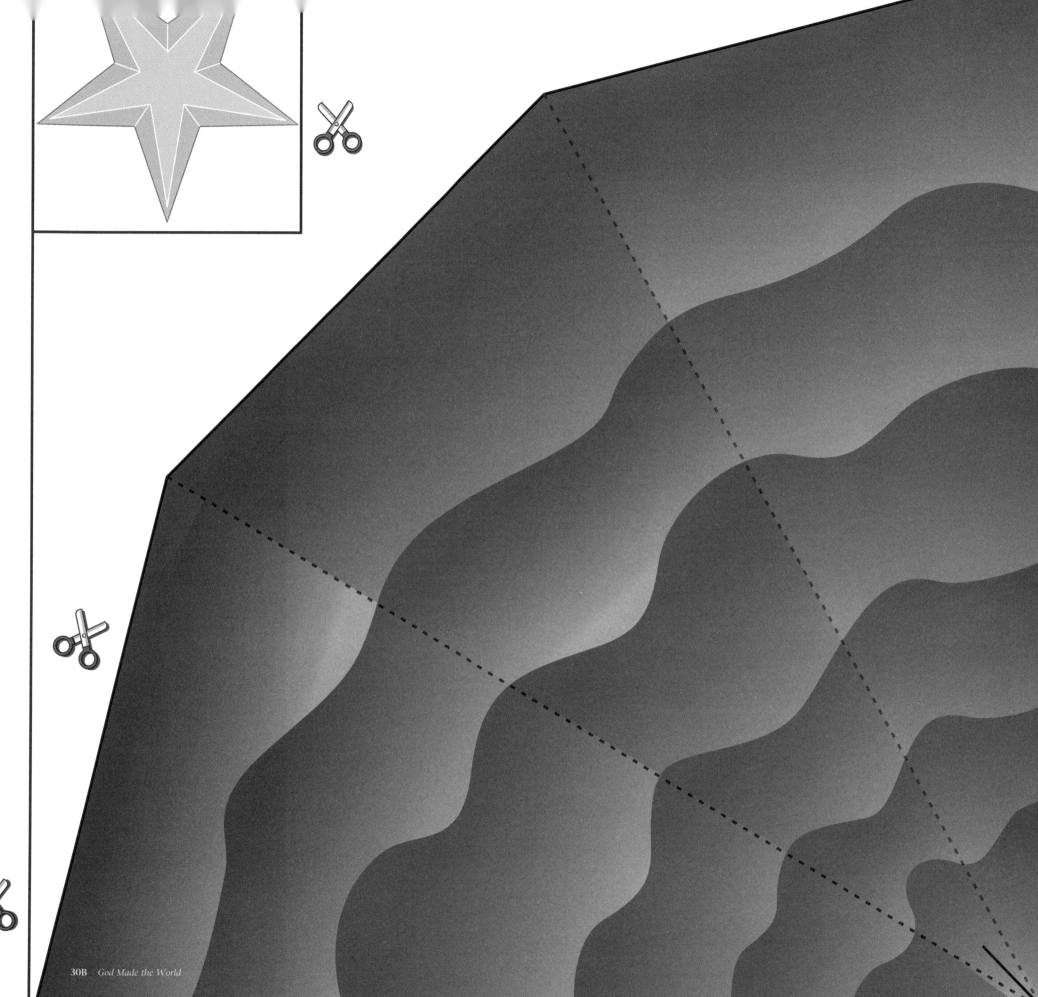

Christmas

Find and circle the five hearts.

The children learned that Valentine's Day is a day to show love. They talked about how to show love for other people. They made a special valentine for someone. Give your child a big hug on Valentine's Day.

Children learn how to love in the home. God's love is usually first communicated to them through their parents. Surprise your child sometimes with hugs, kisses, and little gifts. Show appreciation for signs of love from your child.

Suggested activities
- Bake heart-shaped cookies with your child. Decorate them, if you wish, and take some to a neighbor.
- Help your child address and send valentine cards to friends, relatives, and helpers.
- Read to your child *Louanne Pig in the Mysterious Valentine* by Nancy Carlson or *Valentine Friends* by Ann Schweninger.

Name

Valentine's Day

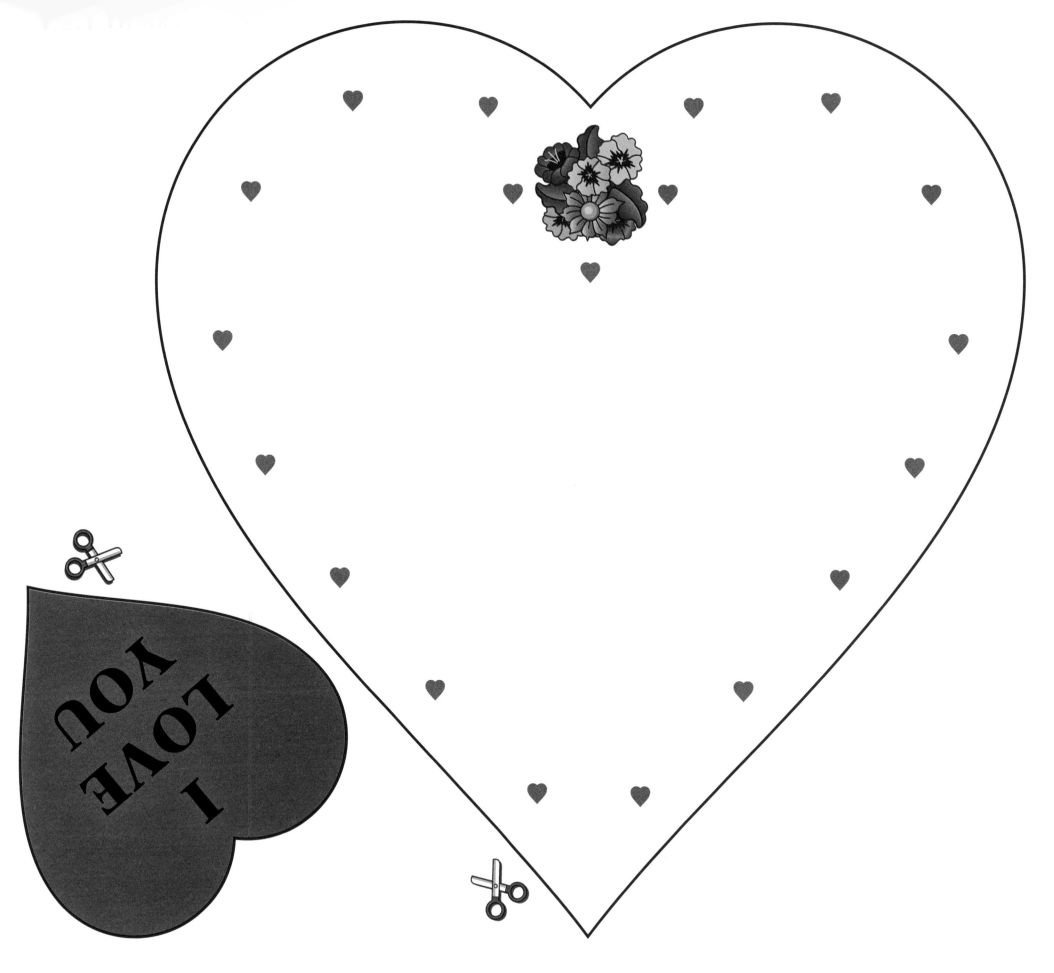

I LOVE YOU

_____

Valentine's Day

God Made the World

Circle what your father does for you.

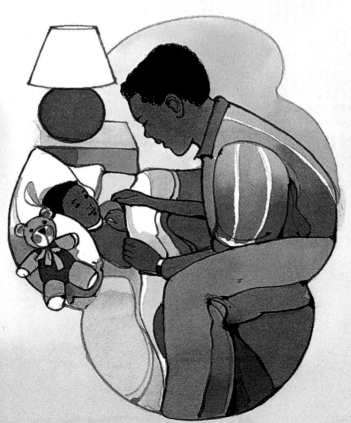

In this lesson the children talked about ways in which fathers show love. They learned that God is our Father in heaven. They were encouraged in return to show love for their fathers by words and actions. Plan ways that your child can be with his or her father in order to grow closer. The child might accompany him to the store, to the barber, or to a sporting event.

Speak to your child about God as a loving Father who cares for us and showers us with gifts.

Suggested activities
- Let your child share in some of the tasks of the father in your family: working in the yard, cleaning the garage, washing windows, cooking.
- Visit, call, or write the grandfathers in your family.
- Have a special meal in honor of the father in your family.
- Read to your child *Daddy Makes the Best Spaghetti* by Anna G. Hines.

Name

Father's Day

You're #1

Happy Father's Day

Thank you—

Love,

_____

Finish coloring this picture.

Family Time

In this lesson the children talked about the coming summer activities. They also recalled what they have learned in preschool. Ask your child to show you the certificate he or she received in class. Congratulate your child and display the certificate.

Suggested activities
- Continue to pray spontaneously with your child during the summer as you enjoy beautiful times together.
- Plan family activities, such as a picnic, games, or attending local festivals and fairs.
- Keep a family scrapbook of the summer's activities.
- Have your family portrait taken.
- Read to your child *A Summer Day* by Douglas Florian.

Name _____

This is to certify that

_____

has completed the *God Made the World*
program of the preschool Christ Our Life Series.

_____
Teacher's/Principal's Signature

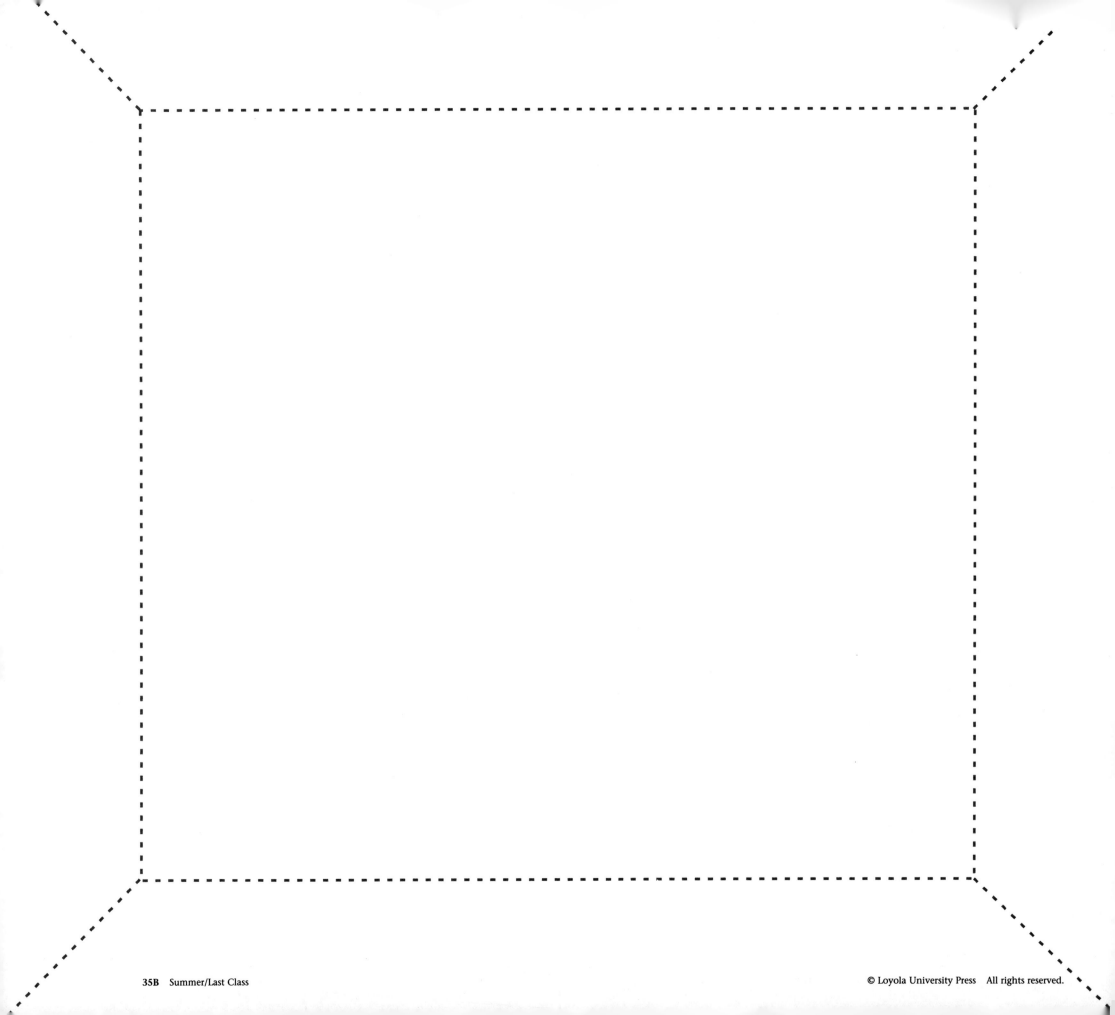

35B   Summer/Last Class

To the tune of "Happy Birthday":
God, we thank you for life.
God, we thank you for life.
Our life is your good gift.
God, we thank you for life.

Lesson 28

Hush! The world is waiting—	[Raise finger to lips.]
Waiting for Baby Jesus.	[Rock arms.]
Mary and Joseph are waiting—	[Extend one arm, then the other.]
Waiting for Mary's Son.	[Rock arms.]
Shepherds and kings are	
waiting—	[Extend one arm, then the other.]
Waiting for the newborn king.	[Rock arms.]
I am waiting—	[Point to self.]
Waiting for my Savior.	[Extend arms up.]

    Mary Kathleen Glavich, S.N.D.

Lesson 29

Turkey Time
Thanksgiving Day will soon be here;
It comes around but once a year.
If I could only have my way,
We'd have Thanksgiving every day!

Lesson 31

Love, Love

Love, love, love, love, Chris-tians this is your _ call. Love your neigh-bor as your-self, for God loves us all.

The Family Card

Enjoy reciting, performing, or singing the following poems, finger plays, and songs at home to review or enrich what your child has learned in preschool.

Lesson 1

To the tune of "Twinkle, Twinkle, Little Star":

Twinkle, twinkle, little star,	[Open and close fists raised high.]
God has made us what we are.	
Though a million stars I see,	[Sweep arms from left to right.]
You are special just like me.	[Point thumb at self.]
Twinkle, twinkle, little star,	[Open and close fists raised high.]
God has made us what we are.	

    Mary Kathleen Glavich, S.N.D.

I Have Two Eyes

I have two eyes that wink and blink,	[Wink.]
I have a mind to make me think,	[Point to head.]
I have two hands that clap for fun,	[Clap.]
I have two feet that jump and run,	[Jump and run in place.]
I have two ears to hear a song,	[Cup ears with hands.]
Two lips to praise God all day long,	[Point to lips.]
I have a body strong and good,	[Put hands out at sides.]
To use for Jesus as I should.	

Lesson 3

To the tune of "Did You Ever See a Lassie?":
The more we are together, together, together,
The more we are together, the happier we'll be.
For your friends are my friends,
And my friends are your friends.
The more we are together, the happier we'll be.

Lesson 5

To the tune of "Row, Row, Row Your Boat":

Women, men, girls, and boys,	[Point to several people.]
Mary, saints, and me—	[Point up and then to self.]
All are members of God's Church.	[Extend arms wide.]
We're God's family.	[Clap twice at the end.]

    Mary Kathleen Glavich, S.N.D.

Lesson 6

Here is the church.	[Interlace fingers, fold hands, knuckles on top, thumbs together pointing up.]
Here is the steeple.	[Point index fingers up, tips touching.]
Open the doors,	[Turn hands over with fingers still interlaced.]
See all the people.	[Wiggle fingers.]

Lesson 8

His Banner over Me Is Love

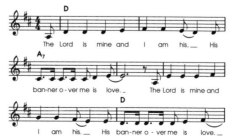

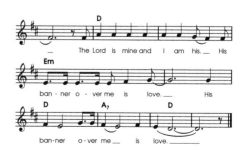

The Lord is mine and I am his,_ His ban-ner o-ver me is love._ The Lord is mine and I am his._ His ban-ner o-ver me is love.

Lesson 9

To the tune of "Here We Go 'Round the Mulberry Bush":
This is the way we wash our clothes,
wash our clothes, wash our clothes.
This is the way we wash our clothes,
with the gift of water.

2. **This is the way we water the yard . . .**
3. **This is the way we brush our teeth . . .**
4. **This is the way we quench our thirst . . .**
5. **This is the way we cook our food . . .**
6. **This is the way we swim in the pool . . .**

Lesson 11

Song: "He's Got the Whole World"
1. **He's got the whole world in his hands.** (four times)
2. **He's got the towering mountains in his hands.**
3. **He's got the peaceful valleys in his hands.**
4. **He's got the busy cities in his hands.**
5. **He's got the lovely farmlands in his hands.**
6. **He's got the hot, dry deserts in his hands.**

Lesson 12

The wind tells me,	[Sway.]
The birds tell me,	[Flap arms.]
The Bible tells me too,	[Open hands like a book.]
How much our Father loves us all,	[Stretch out arms.]
And now I'm telling you!	[Point to self and then point out.]

Lesson 13

Rise and Shine

Lesson 16

This is my garden.	[Extend hand, palm up.]
I'll rake it with care.	[Make pulling motion with hands.]
And plant some flower seeds	[Make planting motions with thumb and index finger.]
Right in there.	
The sun will shine,	[Make circle with arms above head.]
The rain will fall.	[Flutter fingers downward.]
And my garden will blossom	[Cup hands; raise them slowly.]
And grow straight and tall.	

Lesson 18

[Add snapping gestures with thumb and fingers of one hand when the turtle snaps.]
There was a little turtle. He lived in a box.
He swam in a puddle. He climbed on the rocks.
He snapped at a mosquito. He snapped at a flea.
He snapped at a minnow, and he snapped at me.
He caught the mosquito. He caught the flea.
He caught the minnow, but he didn't catch me.

Lesson 19

Thank you for the world so sweet,	[Put out right hand.]
Thank you for the food we eat,	[Put out left hand.]
Thank you for the birds that sing,	[Raise hands.]
Thank you, God, for everything.	[Extend hands to side.]

Lesson 20

[Put hands together with thumbs crossed and "swim."]
I am a fish in the great blue sea.
God made me as happy as can be.
I swim all day and sleep all night.
To be God's fish is my delight.
  Mary Kathleen Glavich, S.N.D.

Lesson 21

To the tune of "Happy Birthday":
God our Father, thank you
For all that you do.
You're full of surprises.
How much we love you!
  Mary Kathleen Glavich, S.N.D.

Little Arabella Miller
Little Arabella Miller
Found a woolly caterpillar.
First it crawled upon her mother,
Then upon her baby brother.
All said, "Arabella Miller,
Take away that caterpillar!"

Lesson 22

The elephant goes like this and that.	[Hold one hand over the other and sway arms from side to side.]
He's oh, so big, and he's oh, so fat.	[Curve arms outward.]
He has no fingers, and he has no toes.	[Hold hand in front with fingers closed.]
But goodness gracious, what a nose!	[Extend arms up with fingers intertwined.]

Lesson 25

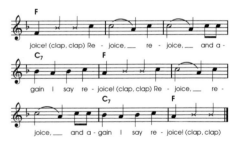

Rejoice in the Lord Always
(Round)

Philippians 4:4

Trace your hand in the center section. Your thumb becomes the turkey's head and neck; your four fingers become tail feathers. (You might purchase real feathers at a craft store.) Add legs. Color or paint the turkey. Fold back the two sides on the dotted gray lines.

Card 30B   Christmas tree
Put round stickers or star stickers on the tree, being careful not to put them on the lines. If you do not have stickers, paint or color decorations. You might add glitter and sequins. Cut out the tree and the square with the star. Cut a slit at the top of the tree on the heavy black line. Fold the tree on the dotted gray lines and tape or staple it together. Insert the star into the slit at the top.

Card 31B   Valentine
Cut out the two hearts. Print your name on the back of the white heart. Punch holes in the small hearts around the edge of the white heart. Go into the first hole under the flowers with red yarn or ribbon, leaving a tail of about five inches. Sew around the heart. Tie the ends of the yarn or ribbon to make a bow. Paste the small red heart in the middle of the white heart. You may wish to omit punching holes and sewing the cards. Give the valentine to someone you like.

Card 32B   Reversible Easter card
Color the sun yellow. Fold the sides of the card forward to cover the sun. Open the card to show darkness giving way to the sun. Fold the sides the other way so that the card shows an egg and, when the sides are opened, a chick.

Card 33B   Mother's Day scroll
Print your name on the line. Color or paint the flowers. Roll up the scroll. Tie yarn or ribbon around the scroll to hold it together. Give it to your mother on Mother's Day.

Card 34B   Father's Day card
Draw a picture in the frame of something your father does for you. Sign your name. Fold the card to stand up. Give the card to your father on Father's Day.

The Family Craft Card
If an activity is to be done at home, help your child follow the directions.

Card 1   Name tag
Cut out the star and print your name on it. Decorate the star with crayons or markers. Add glitter. Punch a hole in the star and string yarn or ribbon through it. Tie the ends together and put the name tag on.

Card 2C   Gift for the family
Print your name at the bottom. Make a picture or design using a sponge held with a clip clothespin and dipped in paint. Or glue on pieces of fabric or torn tissue paper.

Card 3B   Flower
Print your name under the words "I love you." Color the flower (or staple a few circles of colored tissue paper to the center and pull them up around the staple). Cut off the stem and then cut the line between the flower and leaves. Finish cutting out the flower. Paste the leaves and flower to the stem.

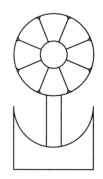

Card 4B   Card for a helper
Fold the card in half. Inside the card draw a picture of the person who helps you and print your name.

Card 5B   Photo frame of God's family
Cut out and paste the pictures of Mary and the other Church members in the matching spaces. Draw yourself in the last space. Keep the extra picture of Jesus as a reminder to love as Jesus loves.

Card 6B   Church
Cut off the strip of pictures and cut apart the altar and the cross. Paste the cross in place on the back of the card. Paste the altar in front of the priest. Fold the church in thirds so that it stands. Cut the doors on the black lines and fold them on the dotted lines so that they open.

Card 7B   Letter from God
Cut off the side strip. Write your name on the front and back of the letter. Fold the letter and tape it closed.

Card 8B   Banner
Cut the banner apart from the long piece of paper. Cut the banner along the diagonal lines and decorate it. Starting with one corner, roll the green strip of paper around a pencil to make a stick. Tape it together and shake out the pencil. Tape or staple the banner to the "stick."

Card 9B   Water scene
Dip pieces of blue yarn in a mixture of water and white glue. Squeeze each piece through your fingers to get rid of the excess glue and arrange it on the paper to look like curvy waves. Add glitter to represent light on the water.

Card 10B   Place mat
Decorate the mat by dipping an old toothbrush in paint and rubbing it over an old wire strainer or screen. Or make designs on the mat using the end of a pencil eraser or glue-stick tube dipped in paint. Cut fringe around the sides or make the sides wavy or jagged.

Card 11B Earth mobile
If you wish, cut out Earth. Draw or paste pictures of land features in the four sections on the back of the card. Punch a hole in the top of the mobile. String yarn or ribbon through the hole to form a loop.

Card 12B Kite
Draw designs or pictures on the yellow part. Cut off the strip at the side and the white triangle at the bottom. Fold the two blue sides to meet in the back and tape them together. Staple or tape the strip to the bottom for a tail. Attach string. Run with the kite to make it fly.

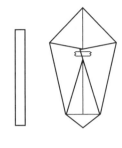
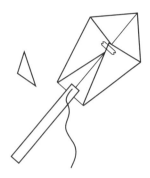

Card 13B Candle
Color the flowers. Print your name on the line above the flowers. Cut off the strip with the flame on it. Roll the large piece of the card and paste or staple it together. Paste the flame to the top of the candle.

Card 14B Book of colors
Fold the card in half. On each page color the picture the same color as the balloon beside or above it. Draw more things that are the colors of each balloon.

Card 15B Weather wheel
Cut off the strip of pictures. Make slits in the wheel with a sharp knife or pointed scissors. Color the sun yellow. Fold the card with the wheel so that it stands. Put the ends of the strip through the slits in the wheel so that the strip can slide back and forth, showing pictures. Change the wheel to match the day's weather.

Card 16B Basket of flowers
Color the flowers. Cut off the strip at the side, which is the handle. Staple one end of the strip to the corner of the large square where there is a blue dot. Staple the other end to the opposite corner so that the ends of the square are pulled up to form a basket. Give the basket to someone you love.

Card 17B Tree
Add leaves to the tree in one of these ways: 1) draw them with crayons or markers; 2) dip sponges in paint and press them on the branches; 3) paste on torn construction paper, fabric, pieces of green tissue paper, or tissue paper of various fall colors; or 4) paste on real leaves.

Card 18D Animal box
Cut out the four yellow squares. Fold up the sides of the box so that the green is inside. Tape the ends together. Fold the yellow squares along the diagonal and stand the animals in the box.

Card 19B Bird mobile
Cut apart the three sections. Tape an end of a piece of yarn to each bird. Tape the other ends of the yarn to the strip. Punch a hole in the top of the strip. Thread yarn through the hole and tie it to make a loop for hanging.

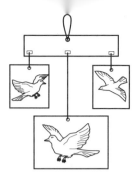

Card 20B Fish picture
Decorate the large fish with crayons or markers. Place the card in a box with a marble that has been dipped in white tempera. Tilt the box from side to side so that the marble leaves tracks that make a net.

Card 21B 3-D butterfly picture
Cut off the side strip and cut out the two butterflies. Fold them on the dotted lines. Color the flower. Put paste on the white part of the wings of the two butterflies and place the butterflies on the picture.

Card 22C Thank-you card for God
Decorate or draw pictures on the card. Print your name on it. (Parents may print "Thank you, God" on the card.)

Card 23B Pet pocket
Cut apart the four pet cards and fold them so that they stand. Cut out the pocket and fold it on the gray dotted line. Staple or paste the sides of the pocket together. Put the pets inside. Add a four-inch piece of yarn as a pet worm.

Card 24B A country's flag
Choose a flag and draw it in the space above the flags. Cut off the section with the many flags. Roll the long piece of paper up to your flag and tape or staple it to form a stick. If you prefer, draw the flag on the longer piece of paper and tape it to a straw, pencil, or ice-pop stick. Tell your child which country's flag he or she has chosen.

Card 25B Clown hat
Cut out the hat and bend and staple it to make a cone. Staple or tape two pieces of yarn to the hat—one at each square—for ties. If you wish, staple or tape a pom-pom to the top.

Card 26B Accordion birthday book
Cut the strips apart on the black line. Fold the strips on the dotted lines so that the lines on the front of the card are on the peaks. Place pages 2 and 3 next to each other and tape them together. Fold back pages 2 and 3 so that they are face-to-face. Fold up the book.

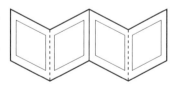

Card 27B Crown
Print your name on the line after "ST." Cut out the crown and the strip of paper. Staple the strip to one end of the crown. Put on the crown and staple the other end of the strip to it so that the crown fits. If you wish, add glitter or sequins.

Card 28B Manger
Cut in on the four black lines. Fold down the edge with the star to meet the other star. Fold down the edge with the flower to meet the other flower. Fold the four sides so that they stand. Overlap the ends and tape them together. Use yellow yarn or strips of paper for straw.

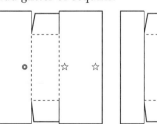

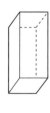